The Universe, All at Once

THE ARAB LIST

Salim Barakat's poetry infused a fresh fervour in both forms and themes of contemporary Arab poetry, while his prose revived stunning narratives where the fantastic becomes a powerful fabric to recreate reality. Huda J. Fakhreddine's *The Universe, All at Once* is not only a very welcome breakthrough in introducing more of Barakat's poetry in English but also a brave and highly commended endeavour in defying the untranslatable.

—*Subhi Hadidi, Syrian literary critic, editorialist and translator*

The dazzlingly enchanting Kurdish-Syrian poet and novelist, and a master of Arabic style, Salīm Barakāt is rumoured to be one of the most enigmatic, riddle-ridden, vorticular writers in modern Arabic literature. Following the tradition of 'minor literature', i.e. writers who choose not to write in their mother tongue but to explore the uncharted terrains of the language of the self-proclaimed majority, Barakāt's grand, incomparable Arabic style is simply untranslatable. Or so we thought. And here comes Huda Fakhreddine and performs—for the second time—the impossible 'task': she doesn't only give these auto-selections from Barakāt's poetry a graceful, exquisite English 'afterlife', in the Benjaminian sense, but gives us new keys to his old secrets, opens up new doors into his seemingly sealed world, and entices the magician himself to talk about his craft.

—*antón shammás, Palestinian writer, poet and translator*

Salim Barakat

The Universe, All at Once

SELECTED POEMS

POEMS SELECTED BY SALIM BARAKAT
TRANSLATED BY HUDA J. FAKHREDDINE

FOLLOWED BY
AN INTERVIEW WITH THE POET

LONDON NEW YORK CALCUTTA

The Arab List
SERIES EDITOR
Hosam Aboul-Ela

Seagull Books, 2024

First published in English translation by Seagull Books, 2024

ISBN   978 1 8030 9 403 8

British Library Cataloguing-in-Publication Data
A catalogue record for this book is available from the British Library

Typeset by Seagull Books, Calcutta, India
Printed and bound in the USA by Integrated Books International

Contents

SELECTIONS FROM

The Five Hundred Fragments

1

Guess what I'm guessing.
This is the last lantern,
and its flame feeds
on the oil of madness.

2

Set beauty aside on the couch,
next to your hearts, the ones you put in bags and set aside on the couch.
This is the tugging of days by their hair.
This is the tugging of lightning by its hair.
This is the tugging of meanings by their intimate hairs.

3

Water warned me not to trust it,
but I hear the clamour of those who believe
in the dominion of waves over the shore,
the ones fascinated by the dominion of rock and sand over the shore,
the dominion of wet spirits over the shore.
I hear the clamour of those fascinated by water's sublime humility
in the sanctuary of its nautical voice.

15

There is no time for one to dismount from tragedy. So put everything aside. The road leading to infinite longing is paved and short.

21

To cross the mountains is to cross through words the poets have forgotten.

22

What did you steal when you were boys like me?
Did you steal eggs from the gods' chicken coop
or candy from the goddesses' shop?
Was it chalk from the monks' school of prose,
dirt from the sorcerers' garden,
or traffic-signs off the roads of murder?
Or was it a wound? Did you steal a wound
that captures the essence of all wounds?

23

These empty beer bottles are full of yesterday's clamour by the sea.
Don't throw them out with trash.

28

Time, too, loses its poise;
it rages and breaks down.

29

Every scarce thing is dangerous.

32

Throw a stone at the sun.
It will fall under the lemon tree.

39

How stunning it is
to stretch out in the skeleton of a ship
where nothing is left
but the exhales of its skipper!

51

The invaders left.
The invaders came.
Let the land prepare to kill itself out of boredom
of minstrels and their songs.

54

With traces of oil on my lower lip,
a glimmer of the morning sun on my bare shoulders,
and a comb in my left hand, I will style Death's short hair
a funny way.

61

The cow is a miracle.
The ram is a miracle.
Asphalt is a miracle, too.
That's how things are.
Directions to the sea are easy to follow, so don't hesitate.
Saddle the void with the saddles of the North
and gather wood for the fireplaces of the murdered,
those who keep vigil, waiting for Earth to set.

63

The prophets' cows, their whales, their boats, their ploughs, their compasses, their pumpkins, and the wells that trail behind them with water-steps, lest they thirst. Their ovens, too, the ones that follow them with fire-steps, lest they hunger.

66

I'm in the same bed
where poetry rests its head
on the pillow of prose.

77

Don't shake the hand
you're capable of breaking.

86

These tweezers,
to pull the word by its tongue.

101

There's beauty that is friend like a dog,
obedient like a dog.
submissive, servile like a dog,
and pisses on every tree trunk
like a dog.

103

The sky sometimes stumbles on the feet of the morning star.

105

Houses of light,
beds of light,
gardens of light,
baths of light,
and pillows of light . . . and there they bury their faces
and suffocate.

108

I don't want a ladder to get me down from the ledge.
I want more despair to keep me where I am,
surviving on the edge.

111

I will pick a fight with the nothing in the room before I leave.
I will pick a fight with the oars of hole-ridden boats,
with myself pouring out of the high priestess' perfume vial,
with those who failed to fill the mangers with fodder
for the armies of cattle.

With the spoiled gardens, I will pick a fight!

113

A mere meter away from Truth, Time fell dead.

122

What is suitable for one fear here, is suitable for every fear over there.

128

Who puts her hand between the other's thighs first:
the sky or the earth.

130

Kindle your body when your heart fails to ignite.

137

Don't misunderstand killing.
Take it to be some longing
or rapture
or the returning of a lost life to its mother.

139

Ghosts
throw their hooks from over a bridge
to catch the cloud fish
reflected in the river.

143

The tongue of coincidence is warm when it licks the popsicles of eternity.

150

One day, I will inherit something:
a suitcase without a handle,
twine to tie my broken bones,
and a cigarette I won't ever smoke.

151

This heart is impetuous,
and this flour betrays the baker.

156

Many are the mistakes of water.

171

When they collide,
clouds leave
black bruises
on the foreheads of other clouds.

174

I know a lot about women:
their shoe sizes,
and their worries.
I know about the bruises they lodge underneath the invisible eyes,
and how the hems of their dresses are scorched when they cross seduction's
    burning terrain.
I know the confusion of patterns on their handkerchiefs every time they wipe
    their hands when their hands cry.
I know the pain they suffer when they fail to block the roads and the kisses
    that diffuse like fragrance.
I know how they smuggle splendour, in their shoes, to the other riverbank.

175

These wounds, these natural reserves.

176

A transgression:
a lilac blooming in a field of irises.

180

Two minutes of time bear resemblance to one little girl.

187

No moaning is louder than the moaning of maps.

197

Ancient famines
stand at the museum doors.

204

Women alone are the crackle of roasting chestnuts.

202

We will keep the letters, sealed and unread.
They are more beautiful sealed,
as a soft touch
we are yet to feel.

210

You were a dog, Moon.
But see! You have become a cat in poems.

211

To fall off a tree, to fall into history.

251

This girl has the vision of a hill,
detecting the flaws of the meadows.

256

What mothers do, fathers do in death.

258

There's a despair that does not surrender its grace.

275

We forgot the ships in our longing for the sea.
We threw ourselves in the sea in our longing for the ships.

288

A hundred mules are not enough
to carry what I do not know to what I know.

292

Seven battles or seventy
do not make a difference in death.

300

Let's build an edifice for noble mistakes.

309

Strangers are kind in the morning,
not in the afternoon.

319

There are dreams
that expel the dreamer.

328

My luck is the luck of the ninth word.
Decipher that if you can!

333

There are no faces under the masks.
Believe the masks!

334

When you don't know what you're being asked,
let the answer turn its other cheek.

335

If you get it wrong in everything, don't give up.
Your only way out is not to give up.
Your only justification is not to give up.
The purity of an honest mistake will be yours
if you don't give up.

337

Don't offend the heart that obsesses
over the tang of sumac in desolate cooking songs.

350

To appease Death's vanity,
pretend to be dead, even if you are not.

370

Death is the engineer of places,
the architect of fear.

371

The howling of wolves, not a fire,
will keep me warm in these woods.

380

I'm not worried about my worries.
I'm worried about what my worries
don't want me to see.

382

Hot-blooded murder:
That's the work of Justice when it trusts in its ethereal balance.

389

The wounded's punch
does not hurt.

391

Between one drop of rain and the drop that follows
is a sorrow—supple and wet.

394

I feel it:
my dying under every tree I pass.

411

The forest resigns its foxes
and demotes its tigers.

413

To take off one's shoes at the entrance to words,
to pull out teeth,
to pluck hairs from the crotch of existence . . .

433

I've been given a war.
I've been given this life, a war.

442

At the turn in the road, burn all that you have.
I've burned a heart or have been burned by one
at every turn.

443

Every framed image deserves shattering.

446

These swollen stones are loaves on time's dinner table.

450

Chaos! Put your head on my thigh.
I believe every killing is innocent.
It's a dilemma. Aren't we all as innocent as glasses of water?

451

The directions have fallen into the traps and their feet are broken.
Months pass like flashes in the rooster's memory.

456

Let's not look for survivors under the rubble yet.
Let them finish singing the national anthem first.

458

Little girl,
religious is the red of your hair!

461

There's nothing's new about devouring hearts that still throb.
These roads are consumable,
these structures consumable,
these systems consumable,
these worlds consumable.
These paper napkins, consumable,
and we, living beings, are all consumed.

474

The little girl,
the quiet little girl yawns
as the caravans crossing the mountain straits pass her by.
Her lips are moist from having drunk.
She leans her left shoulder on that of a cloud, just as little.
Her passing is tender. She drinks from the same cup as the spirits that roam
    the fields, spirits that rise when the plants let their imagination run free.

This little girl was not a little girl.

479

Defeat is not a blow,
not an insult
not humiliation,
not shame.
Every defeat is a justification that the defeated invents,
in praise of the defeat to come.

481

Souls undone,
set aside,
sold as spare parts.

489

When we first saw the sky,
it inspired us to pave roads to it
with the asphalt of death.

492

Be a friend so I can threaten you.
Give me the privilege of a true friendship.
Allow me to threaten you, so I can keep you.

499

This—
the art of living with just one shoe on the right foot.

SELECTIONS FROM

The Grand Ghazal

With hearts or without hearts,
they secretly steal from God
their share of love.
With or without hearts,
they are lovers.

[. . .]

I love them when they leave everything
as it is in the small universe:
the pots,
the cupboard,
the couch and the bed,
untouched.
I love them when they leave the artefacts
in the halls of the small universe
unmoved,
when they preserve the flaws of gold,
when they leave the salt scattered
on the clairvoyant's table,
and the sunset to its squabbles at the door.
I love
the feminine,
careless
of shoes riddled with holes,
of perfection riddled with holes,
of burdens on the backs of souls,
riddled with holes.

And everything remains as it was
since the time of doubt, since the masks of caution,
as it was, since the feminine slipped into the small universe
through the back door.

[. . .]

Careless:
their socks riddled with holes,
their destiny,
their temperament,
their dreams
their will,
their lucky pail
all riddled with holes.

[. . .]

Indifferent:
everything
but the feminine
remains
as it is
in my praise.
They, alone, with an excess of bewilderment, alter the universe.

[. . .]

I love them—having never risked anything before,
not risking anything now
or ever again.

[. . .]

They let slip from their grip
the reins of gardens gone rogue in beauty.
They slam behind them the mundane, a door onto the miraculous, and then
                              each reclines
                              like a sapphire
                              among sapphires.

[. . .]

I love them having toppled the bookshelves. How endearing
that they topple
the bookshelves;
that they collapse kisses like houses over heads,
that they collapse kisses like bridges over boats passing underneath!

[. . .]

Are their bodies bodies or are they houses built on mountain slopes in
    the sky?
I hear their doors slamming, not from the wind but from the flirtations
    of the clouds.

[. . .]

I love them when they are fierce like truth,
out of its place,
like an encounter, out of place,
like a heart, out of place,
like time, out of place
like mirrors, out of place,
like the North,
out
of
place,
like fortunes, out of place,
like life stories, current
and out of place.

[...]

like the sky,
out of place.

[...]

I love them unbothered when they are late to exit
from poetry to song.
And they are always late. They never rush into meanings,
always content with the way ash enunciates his names, whispering in their
    ears—their ears of flame.

[. . .]

I love them,
larger than deceit
and smaller than trust.
I love them as clearly as
plump lips,
wave-kissed
and glistening.

[. . .]

I love them without caution, as they fold me,
gather time above me as well as place,
and stack us all one on top of the other like shirts.

[. . .]

I love them without secrets,
transparent like lucid words spoken hastily.

[. . .]

I love them
barefoot,
not bothered by the earth,
muddy
or gravelly,
or sandy.
I love them indifferent to the earth
when it cracks, craving prophecies.

[. . .]

I love them,
trapped in the straits of the night,
unable or unwilling to escape.
I love them like that, greedy perhaps,
with hearts as beds,
hearts as chimneys,
hearts as fertile as pain.
I love them like that,

tormented like two geese for whom one lake is not enough,
I love them trembling with what I do not know,
moderate in slaughter
whenever they stumble upon a history.

I love how they chatter when victorious
and chatter when defeated.
I love how they throw obsessions at each other,
It's funny how they only nap in the shelter of howling,
roaring places.

I love them, unversed in the flirtations of the morning,
and on their shoulders, as they pass by wars, are the same old jugs—
    vinegar jugs.
I love them shy like the third line in every notebook,
cautious to discuss the dispute between the door and the window,
between beauty and its brother.
Their shoulders slouch slightly,
and the places of hearts in their chests remain unknown.
They are doubtful,
wary of everyone,
suspecting betrayal
at every mention
of God.

[. . .]

I love them when they are capable of unforgettable mistakes.
There they are.
Mirrors have disappointed them,
failed to recognize their truths.
I love them, forgotten,
whenever they tried to remind the fire of themselves,
they were remembered by the ash
that still thirsts for the fire's forgetfulness.

[. . .]

I love them when they are peacemaker,
loyal to the regret that precedes war
and the regret that follows it.
I love them when they are late to their own parties.
I love them more when they don't even show up to their own parties.
They rock place once and
it continues to spin for ever.

[. . .]

I love them,
speaking to the wind
with their hands in their pockets,
the hands that pull hearts out from among broken ribs,
hearts that have never been broken,
or the hands that return broken hearts,
to their rightful places
in that elegant void,
among the ribs.

[. . .]

I love them floating on water, unmoored,
no anchors to weigh them down,
and no sails to direct them.
They recline when they speak,
sharing plans on golden plates,
plotting the transfer of hearts
from the encampments of reality
to the fortresses of anger.

I love them when they are the thoughts of trees,
the musings of pavements,
the bleeding of padlocks.
They have been assembled by enigma.
Elated like enigmas,
they swap bridges
between
the sunset
and the unknown.

[. . .]

I love them as drawings within drawings,
lined up, one dimension after the other,
until form is exhausted
and colour shredded
by the claws of colour.

[. . .]

I love them when they know a lot
about the white of a tired paper, blank like death,
a lot about the wind when it stumbles to make sense,
a lot about bread exhausted by its own folly,
and a lot about deadly climaxes
and the rejuvenating abyss.

I love them
when they know
much that is
unbearable
to know.

[. . .]

I love them when they are a foot beneath reason
or a foot above it,
minutes before illusion
or minutes after it,
an arm's length above reconciliation

or an arm's length below conflict,
a span above the idea
or a span below it,
a heartbeat below fury
or a stone's throw above silence.

[. . .]

I love them,
and they are the familiar
determined to deny
every certainty.

[. . .]

They have gone too far
in the harm they inflicted on Death,
to save it from itself, they say.
And now, Death is like
their keys
that clink
when they open the doors
and head out to the miracle shops.

[. . .]

I love them and they are no return:
ahead is a thread,
and behind is their needle.

They won't rip or mend anything.
As always, after they hang life on its hook in the sand hall,
they hang next to it the hats of fury and the pants of luck,
never to be worn again.

[. . .]

I love them,
when they do not wonder
which to burn first,
the bridge or the river.

[. . .]

I love them when they sit the wolves of the deep beside them,
and the days like cats nestling at their feet.

[. . .]

I love them when they don't bother to descend to a predicament
but train it to climb up to them,
tamed like a cat.

[. . .]

I love them
full of doubt that is announced
the way faith is announced:
a door slammed
in all
the faces
that were
before.

[. . .]

I love them when they peel the stars
and slice them over every fruit bowl.

I love them turning their backs to the sea,
sipping their beers under beach umbrellas,
content with the purring of the waves behind them,
the waves they tied by their sea-foam necks to the legs of their chairs.

[. . .]

I love them refusing to make peace,
even when the universe
stubbornly explodes.

[. . .]

I love them when they pour their bodies
into their flowing clothes
like meanings
filling words
until
the words
swoon.

[. . .]

I love them when they drown the mirrors with their reflections:
I hear the pleas of the drowning mirrors.
I hear the pleas of the light in the mirrors.

[. . .]

I love them, mischievous,
jostling through the crowd, shouldering their way through,
quarrelling with themselves, first;
with the daylight, first;
with the garments that fail to define their shapes, first;
with the nursing rocks and the suckling light, first;
with the chiefs of space and the lords of sound, first;
quarrelling with the shadows, first, the shadows that hang like wide
    sleeves on their shirts, first.

[. . .]

I love them when they turned to the earth and stitched it into the hems of
    their dresses, when they wrap the directions around their shoulders
    like cloaks.

[. . .]

They are indifferent to deceit that leaves kisses on distrustful lips.
They do not care for lips that spoil the taste of kisses, that are devious
    about the taste of kisses upon them.

They leave the years windless, and the days toppled, feet in the air.

And around them, nothing but sappy poems in praise of the masculine
and his instruments,
bucks butting heads
on the edge
of eternal
ridges.

[. . .]

They trust
what the window
hears
not what
it sees.

[. . .]

I love them when they open to the wind their front doors,
the southern doors of their imagination,
the doors to the number that has not yet found a place
in their deal with the second south,
and the doors to the third north.

[. . .]

They, the feminine,
are an inflection, a hesitation
that dwells in the last beat of
every line of poetry.

SELECTIONS FROM

A Spiritual Admonition

*

The mirrors have been condemned.
They were gathered, and their images were destroyed one by one.
The dimensions slid over their hollowed surfaces.
They were emptied of their powers to reveal, whether concave or convex.
The mirrors were released. Nothing reflected in them but voices. Damn it!
Damned be the images and us, the echoes of images.

*

Believe in the days
with broken fingers,
the months
with broken feet,
and the years
with broken hips.

Look to the sky:
It is a poem that was hastily written yesterday. Damn it!
Damn haste and its warmth!
Damn everything cursed and cruel, and sweet too.

*

The desolate days embrace each other under the coffee tree,
and those tame ones next to us are prophets oblivious of their departed
followers,
or enemies whose pockets are so tight that whenever they pull their hands
out, they pull them skinned. Damn it!
Damn their merciful madness.
Damn this uninheritable madness.

*

Here we are free like a wound,
free like folly,
a little or much like death. Seven feet away from life,
we are not the way death desired us to die. Damn it!
Is this how we spite death, by dying seven feet away from life?
Damn this death,
a phone ringing
in no one's pocket!

*

Should we forgive?
We are incapable of forgiveness,
yet we cannot deny what we see:
the negation of windows, at times,
the negation of doors, at times,
the negation of homes, at times,
the negation of all place, all the time.

*

A calm descends after the massacre:
a chance to arrange the scattered things,
to pick up the crushed shards,
and smooth out the rugs ruffled on the battle floor.

*

We prepared to pull the pavements from under their feet,
to pull reward and punishment from under their feet,
to pull meaning from under their feet,
to pull the present and the future from under their feet,
to pull sunrise and sunset from under their feet,
to pull what's ahead and what's behind from under their feet,
to pull the human, finally, from under their feet.
Damn it! And yet,
here we find ourselves,
with our feet buckled under our feet.

*

Who's to blame the lightning today?
Who will chastise it?
Damn this lightning
that betrays the timid madness
concealed beneath
the cloaks of fear!

*

There are no stations in the universe
for the trains to stop,
no station for time that rolls on its steel wheels
down the steel tracks
to stop.

Damn this universe
that slyly steals glances
at our dinner plates!

*

Neither staying
nor leaving comforts.
Places are sure to deceive in saffron-flavoured ways,
like the anger of cups,
like history retiring to bed without its history,
like lightning ravished in the wild lands.
Damned be all places!
Nothing out there but the panting of the fugitive
who trades his voice for that of the auctioneer.
Damned be the places, cynically wagging their tails,
and growling like whirlpools beneath the ships.

SELECTIONS FROM

A Battle in Aquatime

*

These ruins are familial,
this wreck familial
this bleeding and these massacres familial,
the slaughterhouses familial,
and these poems, they are familial too,
and their meanings stale.

We ascend to a sky collapsing on top of another sky,
and this, our pagan digging in search of a god in the mines of thunder.
I will end the ancestors. I will rid myself of the ancestors, tattered and frayed
like bits of cloth. Not even history can sew them together, despite its needles
    of anthems and songs.
I will rid myself of the ancestors, sliced like pieces of bread on which history
    hasn't managed to spread its butter at breakfast.

*

Tea, cold in pots,
days, locked in bathhouses, and the days still bathing inside,
fortunes, stumbling over the cats that sleep in epics,
countries, escaping from their people,
and that's no wonder at all.
There's no wonder in a torn body
but in the shirt torn upon the body.

I will end the hours whose feet are bound with wires to the table legs.
I will end the thoughts that are without consequences,
without shoes,
without rings or necklaces,
the thoughts that wander nervously in narrow words.
I will end the existence
that avoids
being touched.

*

Here are the heirs of the bull hearts
and the tyrants who are kind to gardens.

The gardeners guide the bees to the pollen in the gods' blossoms.
Sweat drips
on the forehead
of the years
and the years' hands tremble.
I will end what happened to the horse
and what happened to the earth stretching beneath the horse's hooves.

I will end all that robs me of my feeling as a stranger.
A stranger I will remain,
and strangers are content
with the magic of their sorrow.

An Interview with Salim Barakat

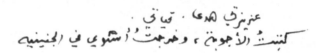

*'Dear Huda, I've answered your questions
and I'm off to barbeque in the garden.'*

HUDA J. FAKHREDDINE. How do you remember yourself as a child?

SALIM BARAKAT. I was probably never a child. I never walked the ground with child's feet. The adults around us forced us to be men—old men even. As children, we led lives that lacked a true sense of existence.

HUDA. What is the most memorable moment from your childhood?

SALIM. The ups and downs of our financial situation is what I remember. My father was a seasonal grain merchant and was not particularly interested in saving money or planning for the future. Our family experienced periods of prosperity followed by financial hardships. It was traumatic to live a comfortable life one year and then be thrust into dire poverty the next. I did not feel secure as a child. Even today, I wake up frightened by the memories of that past.

HUDA. Was there a relationship that had the biggest impact on you in your family?

SALIM. Yes. The crowdedness in the house. The household was chaos with no traffic signs.

HUDA. How would you describe your relationship with your mother—what is her name? What remains of her in your memory?

SALIM. My mother's name is Fattoum (a nickname for Fatima). I do not remember her very well, but I shall never forget her fondness for sweets, especially for shʿaibiyyāt and qatayif (popular desserts made with dough and sugar syrup, often served with nuts). I had to chase the travelling sweets-seller to buy those for her. He carried the large metal tray on his head and roamed the streets. He would tire me out.

I also remember my mother's fondness for fried chard with onions. Every spring, I had to wander in the wilderness with a basket and a small knife in search of the wild plant. A large basketful of this plant once fried was barely enough to fill one plate. Yes, I remember how I spent hours in the wilderness, day after day, harvesting chard for my mother.

HUDA. What was your relationship like with your father?

SALIM. There was nothing special. My father was a simple, religious man who was preoccupied with feeding all eleven of us. Sometimes,

I accompanied him on hunting trips. He'd bring his 12-mm gun. Unfortunately, he was not good at hunting.

HUDA. How many brothers and sisters do you have?

SALIM. We are nine. Four sisters, four brothers and I.

HUDA. What was your relationship like as siblings?

SALIM. It was like a circus. Eleven people in a two-room house, a wide yard, and an olive tree that never grew.

HUDA. What has survived of your relationship with your brothers and sisters?

SALIM. Nothing. They are closer to each other than they are to me. I left the house in my early twenties, driven by rebellion and the need to escape the suffocation of that house. Today, my brothers and sisters are scattered across the globe—two of them have found refuge in heaven, where we hope souls find shelter.

I have a sister who is still in Qamishli and another who has been in Sweden for forty years (I only saw her once twenty years ago). There's one sister in Lebanon, another in Egypt, a brother in Germany, and a brother who recently came to Sweden as a refugee. Two brothers have been missing for more than forty years; they were arrested by the Syrian regime, and then disappeared.

HUDA. When did you leave home for the first time?

SALIM. I left Qamishli for Damascus in 1970. My family later joined me. A year and a half later, I left them and escaped to Beirut.

HUDA. Do you remember the last meeting with your parents? Where and when was it?

SALIM. We had met in Beirut, in 1977. It was actually the first and last meeting since I had left Syria.

HUDA. What do you remember from the village?

SALIM. What remains in my memory of the village is what remains in my memory of myself. Am I not the memory of the village? I am not a villager, but I am most likely a village.

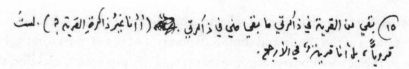

'What remains in my memory of the village . . .'

HUDA. How do you recall your first visit to Damascus? What were the circumstances?

SALIM. Damascus was the escape to the 'big world'. I was driven by all my obsessions with art and freedom. To me, Damascus, the capital city, meant all the writers, the newspapers, the magazines and the publishing houses I had dreamt of. And, how miserable my dream was! I found the city rather dreary and repressed in every way. The fear of authority was palpable, there was panic in the air. I needed the violence of freedom, so I left for Beirut after a year and a half in Damascus—the bleeding wound.

When the capital city bleeds, it means that the whole country is a wound, and we are nothing but wounds walking on feet.

إنّ تنزف العاصمة ُ يكُنّ البلدُ لم في نزيف ٍ من جُرح هنا- لمن المردم ماشيتة على الأقدام

'When the capital city bleeds . . .'

HUDA. What did you read at home?

SALIM. My father had a small collection of religious books—a few interpretations of the Quran and some Sufi poetry. But I used to read everything in the school library; and the translated fiction, mostly classics, that were collected by my cousin who was obsessed with them. And of course, I devoured all the modern poetry at the cultural centre in Qamishli. These were my early sources.

HUDA. What are some of the favourite novels you read in translation?

SALIM. It's a long list. Melville's *Moby Dick*, Victor Hugo's *The Hunchback of Notre Dame*, Mitchel's *Gone with the Wind*, Harriet Beecher Stowe's *Uncle Tom's Cabin*, Alexandre Dumas's *The Three Musketeers*, Kafka's *The Castle*, Scott's *Ivanhoe*, Woolf's *Orlando* and *The Waves*, Dostoyevsky's *The Brothers Karamazov*, Dickens' *A Tale of Two Cities* and *Oliver Twist*, Emily Brontë's *Jane Eyre*, Charlotte Brontë's *Wuthering Heights*, Lewis Carroll's *Alice in Wonderland* and Hawthorne's *The Scarlet Letter*. These are but some of the classics.

Of course, I was also very keen on reading the novels by Nobel laureates like Faulkner's *The Sound and the Fury*, Steinbeck's *The Grapes of Wrath*, Buck's *The Good Earth*, Pasternak's *Doctor Zhivago*, Camus's *The Stranger*, Zweig's *Letter from an Unknown Woman* and the list goes on.

HUDA. Which languages did you speak at home?

SALIM. We only spoke Kurdish.

HUDA. What was school like?

SALIM. School? You mean hell. Children usually complain about going to school, even if they go to the best school. Can you imagine going to a slaughterhouse of humiliation? Sometimes I close my eyes and imagine myself as a bulldozer demolishing every school I ever entered.

HUDA. Your family spoke Kurdish and the Arabic school was hell—why did you decide to write in Arabic then?

SALIM. There were no Kurdish books available to me, and the spoken Kurdish did not tempt me to write. Moreover, Kurdish was banned in Syria. My father's small library had only two books related to Kurdish —one was a Kurdish translation of al-Busiri's *The Mantle Ode*, the famous thirteenth-century Arabic poem praising the prophet, and the second was an Arabic translation of Ahmad Khani's *Mem and Zin*, a seventeenth-century Kurdish epic poem.

HUDA. At what age did you start thinking about writing? Do you remember the first text you wrote?

SALIM.: I had written some poems when I was fifteen—influenced by the classical poetry. The creative spark was first kindled at the age of seventeen with a poem titled 'Nashīd al-anshād al-ḥuzayrānī' (The June Song of Songs) in 1968. I had almost fainted with joy when it was published in the *al-Thawrah* newspaper, on half a page with a drawing by the famous artist Nazir Nabʿah.

HUDA. Do you remember any lines from the poem?

SALIM. I only remember the first line. 'Your fiery face, my lady, is ice and spears.'

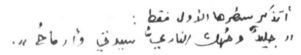

'I only remember the first line . . .'

HUDA. How did this poem come to be published in the newspaper?

SALIM. It wasn't difficult. I had submitted the poem from Qamishli to *al-Thawrah* in Damascus and they published it—just like that, without any formal introduction or pervious contact. The literary editor was one of the famous poets at the time. I forget who it was though.

HUDA. What were the readings that led to your first compositions? Do you have a friend among the pre-modern poets who influenced you at the time and to whom you find yourself returning even today?

SALIM. I liked to read Abu Nuwas at the time, then Abu Tammam. But for a long time since then, I haven't been inclined towards any of them.

HUDA. Why? Have you stopped reading pre-modern poetry?

SALIM. I haven't stopped reading, but I've stopped leaning towards any particular poet from the classical tradition since I became more interested, and invested, in modern poetry and its revelations.

HUDA. How did you spend the year and a half in Damascus? Were you studying or working? What did you take away from your experience?

SALIM. I was supposed to study Arabic literature at the university, but my passion for and obsession with poetry became my true calling. I rebelled and got carried away with drinking, relationships and poetry competitions, and all that distracted me from university. I did not attend a single class!

Then came the final awakening blow—the regime. Back then, every policeman in Damascus carried a pair of scissors in his pocket and was given the authority to 'discipline deviants' by cutting young men's hair when it was perceived to be inappropriately long. The freedom we dreamt of in poetry was met with scissors of censorship, too. I had no choice but to escape to Lebanon, in search of freedom. The first thing I did when I got there was to wear my hair long, down to my shoulders.

I even had a photograph of me with Mahmoud Darwish, both of us with long hair. It was taken by the journalist Samir al-Sayegh in 1973 at Adonis' house. My younger brother had borrowed photo, and later when I asked for it, he said that the Syrian police had raided our house and confiscated it along with other items that belonged to an older brother of ours, who was active against the regime. The brother disappeared as did the photograph, never to be seen again. He was killed, as was another younger brother of mine.

HUDA. Did you arrange to move to Beirut or was it an unplanned escape? Did you have any friends there?

SALIM. I arrange for this final migration with a Syrian-Armenian friend. He left Syria a few months before I did. He rented a small room with a kitchen from people who were originally from the region of Ḥawran in Syria and worked as porters in Beirut. My friend found work at a bakery. Once settled, he sent word to me, and I joined him. This was in 1971 and I have not been back to Syria since.

HUDA. Do you remember your arrival in Beirut, your first encounter with the city? Did you have any connections or acquaintances in the literary scene?

SALIM. When I first arrived in Beirut, I looked for that bakery in Bourj Hammoud, the Armenian suburb where my friend lived. We ate a roasted chicken in a restaurant and drank Pepsi. I remember how sweet it was—a sublime sweetness!

The next day I visited the office of *al-Anwar* newspaper to meet Samir al-Sayegh, who was on the editorial board of *Mawāqif* journal. We knew each other because *Mawāqif* had published my poem 'Qunsul al-atfāl' (The Consul of Children) which I had mailed to them from Damascus. When they received it, Adonis, who was editor-in-chief, wrote to me saying, 'Your poem surprised me, and I am rarely surprised.'

I met Samir al-Sayegh in the office of *al-Anwar* and he took me to Adonis' house. Adonis, Khalida Saʿid and their daughters, were surprised. 'O how young he is!' They all kept saying.

My only prior connection with *Mawāqif* was that poem I had sent in them from Syria. They knew my poetry. And when I arrived in Beirut, they welcomed me.

HUDA. Your first collection, *Kull dākhil sa-yahtif bi-ismī wa kull khārij aydan* (They All Shall Hail Me, Those Who Enter and Those Who Exit) was a thunderous debut. Tell me about the circumstances of publishing this collection? When did you write the poems? Did you deliberately arrange them in a certain way?

SALIM. I wasn't thinking of writing a book when I composed those poems, but Adonis insisted that I put together enough pieces to make a collection. So, I selected the poems myself and designed the cover. That's how my first collection came together, and *Mawāqif* published it. Almost all the Lebanese newspapers and magazines praised the collection. One sentence by the poet and critic Iṣam Maḥfouz still rings in my mind. He opened his review with the line, 'Salim Barakat is a name to memorize.'

HUDA. Describe the book cover that you had designed.

SALIM. It was a collage of yellow paper-clippings with writing in the elegant gold Kufi script, and nestled among them was a photo of me.

HUDA. When did you start taking an interest in painting? Could you tell me about the relationship between your art and your writing.

SALIM. I began painting at the age of fifteen, inspired by two of my friends from school and the neighbourhood—one was Assyrian, and the other Armenian. They were skilled at depicting natural scenes, unlike me. There is a very bad oil-painting of mine hanging on the wall in my older sister's home in Qamishli. It's been almost fifty-eight years, but I think it might still be there!

I stopped painting in Beirut. Then lazily picked it up again in Cyprus. During my time in Sweden, I was diligent for a few years, but eventually gave up. I felt like I wasn't making any progress. Painting requires time, and that I simply don't have.

HUDA. Could you tell us about the poet or the poem that had the deepest impact on you from these early readings in modern poetry?

SALIM. The initial excitement—in the late 1960s—was triggered by the idea of renewal or rejuvenation that we, as rebels, sought to bring about in modern poetry. I read poetry collections that I borrowed from friends and others which I found at the cultural centre in Damascus. The poets we read back then were those who are labelled, due to a lack of critical discernment, as 'pioneers'. They were the subject of our readings before we stumbled upon their sources, such as T. S. Eliot and Ezra Pound. I have written about this in an article published in *al-Hayat* newspaper in 1995. I think it was titled 'Poetry without Pioneers'.

Our writings and experiments stemmed from our deep interest in, or perhaps, fascination with various schools of thought such as Surrealism, Symbolism, Dadaism, Romanticism . . . We devoured everything.

However, I was soon disillusioned with the Arabic modernist movement's claims of renewal. The game of taf`ilah, the experiments with line breaks, and discarding some metrical restrictions were easy moves. The real challenge of innovation required much more than that. The alluring depth of this modernizing project was elsewhere, in the works of American poets as well as the English, the French, the Germans and the Spanish poets.

HUDA. Is your objection to classifying poets of the early modernist movement in Arabic as 'pioneers' due to your discovery of the foreign influences? And does this deny their pioneering role in Arabic poetry?

SALIM. I do not want to appear ungrateful by denying the efforts or pioneering role of some poets in modern Arabic poetry. Among the early generation are both 'pioneering' poets with hesitant steps as well as poets who were still submissive to the old methods. The translations of poetry from other languages that were done in the beginning of the twentieth century revealed that our modernists did not possess a coherent project or vision.

HUDA. Who were the modern poets who caught your attention in the beginning?

SALIM. At first it was Badr Shakir al-Sayyab, the Iraqi poet. Sadly, his life and career were short-lived. Eventually, I became interested in the works of Adonis, Khalil Ḥawi, and even Nizar Qabbani.

HUDA. Adonis supported you in the beginning and had an influence on your early works. How do you relate to him or his work?

SALIM. I admired Adonis when I was young, but later I found his poetry and his approach too easy.

HUDA. What do you mean by 'easy' here?

SALIM. I define ease in writing as a disregard for the reader's critical abilities. This occurs when the author neglects to assess their own poetic integrity before sharing their work. This disregard may stem from arrogance or an assumption that their language and imagination are suffice and will undoubtedly produce something readers will accept, and perhaps even be grateful for. That's what I mean by ease in writing. It's when poets write without concern or anxiety, fuelled by the confidence in their reputation or the credit they already possess with their readers.

HUDA. Is difficulty or ambiguity the counterpart of this ease you're describing? I'm sure you are aware that your writing is often described as difficult. Is that something you aim for?

SALIM. I don't aim to be difficult or deliberately seek complexity. However, my imagination, my relationship to myself—whether clear or ambiguous—and my exploration or interrogation of language, may create a sense of convolution when they converge in a text. I am aware of this. I don't hesitate to push language towards forms or configurations that reveal something already embedded or dormant within it. It is my prerogative to stretch language to its limits. Every creation is a complex construction, and nothing is more intricate or complicated than the simple cell—the origin of all creation.

HUDA. In your first collection, you experimented with meter and rhyme. What did you want to achieve in terms of form in that first book?

SALIM. To speak of form alone is to split the spirit of the poem arbitrarily and violently. The poem is a unity, a whole.

HUDA. OK, perhaps not form, but structure. It's clear that you are occupied with structure and design.

SALIM. A poem is an edifice I strive to build on a deep foundation, steadily expanding upon it—much like adding weighty extensions to a cathedral, without fear of collapse.

HUDA. I'm interested in these cathedrals of yours—the long poems like *Syria* and *al-Abwāb kulluhā* (All the Doors) for example. How do you structure them?

SALIM. I prefer long poems. I have a desire to capture the entire universe, all at once. I know that that is an impossible ambition to set for a text, but I won't give up. I'll keep trying. In novels as well as poems, I want each one of them to be a meticulously designed, yes, like a cathedral. In both poetry and prose, I commit myself to a strict architecture, without compromise. I know my readers well. They are bright. I cannot trick them.

HUDA. How would you define the 'deep foundation' upon which you build your cathedrals? Is it an idea, a linguistic composition, a rhythm?

SALIM. A cathedral in poetry is the expansion of the poem's structure in all directions—upward, inward, sideways . . . and adding embellishments with pillars, arches, windows, bows, chandeliers, domes, balconies, stained glass and friezes. It is a grand design that necessitates the full utilization of the poet's structural toolkit to erect that 'linguistic edifice' —employing all the available instruments of rhythm, construction and imagination.

HUDA. You insist that you have no ancestors in the practice of writing. I don't think that's possible, especially since you're a voracious reader. So why do you resist placing your poetic project in a larger context or legacy of sorts?

SALIM. Why am I never asked about my mother in writing or my tribe of women writers or ancestors? But I understand your question, and I will surprise you. I do have a father who is no one's father really. No matter how much I insist on this lineage, this father will never be mine. He is not a father to begin with. And I can deprive him of his fatherhood. If I want, I can make him my son instead . . .

Let me tell you a story. I was four years old when my cousin took me to the cinema for the first time. It was a western film. Another time we saw a horror film.

After that, I made use of every possible way to save money to go to the cinema. I tried to watch every film. When I went to Beirut, I compensated for the films banned in my country by going to the cinema every single day, without fail. I watched three on Sundays. Except for some days during the civil war, I never slept without watching a film. I do not hesitate to claim that I am a 'film encyclopedia'.

I know that by 'fathers' you meant the works of master writers before me and their influence. I understand that. A week after my arrival in Beirut, I found a job in one of the publishing houses, first as a copy-editor, and shortly thereafter as an editor with Dar Awda, the well-known publisher that produced the collected works of many of the major Arab poets of the time. This gave me access to a treasure trove. As an editor, I was able to buy books from other publishers at a discount. I was voracious like the sea foam which gifts every rock on the shore a little bit of its pain. I had come from a country whose regime was ingeniously adept at forbidding, with its colourful methods of restriction and censorship. Still, the library I had left behind in Syria, while not large, had a selection of seminal works of philosophy, theatre, literature and translated novels by luminaries, and a few poetry collections. In poetry, my taste has always been difficult.

I believe what will surprise you with regards to 'literary lineage' which holds every writer on earth to a belonging or allegiance to an origin of some sort is that I feel deeply connected, in some way, to the magic of cinema. I feel that I owe something to the magic of the moving image when it becomes its own language, when it possesses its unique poetic patterns.

I am aware that in this 'convoluted explanation' of mine I might be staring at death's feet and not his face, but I know my secrets. I know that it's an adventure or perhaps a risk to claim to fashion a father from clippings of images and photographs. But I am convinced that every great film I've seen was a bridge allowing me to crossover to poetry.

HUDA. You have surprised me, indeed. The magic of cinema, as you describe it, is captivating. I did not expect that your source of inspiration would not primarily be linguistic, given that you wield the sword of language and mine its grammar and imagination the way you do.

SALIM. I won't deny that reading poetry is the way to hone the skills of arranging a poetic phrase, finding rhythm and animating words. Committedly reading poetry teaches one the techniques of weaving, but the visual image with its movement and wealth of symbolism is what creates the poeticity of words. A powerful stimulating image is magic. It facilitates the translation emotions into words. The moving image is the original language of human imagination.

I will add to this father-cinema, a mother I find in the narrative prose of the novel. And I don't mean by this poetic-prose or prose with poetic qualities. I mean sternness in description, dialogue and the arrangement of situations. I mean prose that provokes poetry, prose that can condense life into glimpses from which poetry derives its eloquent charm.

I can refer here to the prose of Henry Miller, Tennessee Williams, Virginia Woolf and Edgar Allan Poe—not forgetting to mention prose in the form of painting, the prose of colours and lines.

But I return to the inspiration of the moving image, and specifically to the rapture of the black-and-white in old silent films. I close my eyes and I see the battles in *Ivan the Terrible* (1944) by the Russian director Sergei Eisenstein, the slaughtered horses in scenes from *Napoleon* (1927) by the French director Abel Gance, the dancer in *Metropolis* (1926) by the German director Fritz Lang, the madness of the train scene in *The General* (1926) by the American director Buster Keaton, the gorilla's touching the girl in *King Kong* (1933) by the American directors Merian

C. Cooper and Ernest B. Schoedsack, and countless moments of hysteria in Charlie Chaplin's silent films, not his talkies.

By describing this hidden lineage or debt to cinema—not to literary sources—I do not mean to imply that I am the product of an unusual 'singularity' or that I am exceptionally self-made. I'm pointing to other 'possibilities', nothing more.

There are pathways to what lies beyond the rainbow of 'origins', pathway that hasty criticism in its classification fails to notice. Perhaps I do belong to the nineteenth or the eighteenth century. That's how I feel.

So, who, then, is my father, dear Huda? And which mother is my mother?

هناك مسرّاتٌ إلى ماوراء قوس قَزَح "الأصول" لدينته إليها النقد العجول في التصنيف .
لربما أنتي ، بقّةٌ ، إلى القرن السابع عشرَ أوالثامن عشر . ذاك إحساسي .
مَنْ "أبٍ هو أبي ، ياخِيريَّ هُوى ؟ وأين "أمٌّ "هي أُمي ؟

'There are pathways to what lies beyond . . . mother?'

HUDA. Haven't you found a poet who entices you or captivates you with their imagery the way cinema does?

SALIM. Walt Whitman tempts with his images very much. I find myself attracted to poet-painters like him who create scenes and images in their poetry.

HUDA. What do you think of the phrase 'your poetic project'?

SALIM. Building a universe in poetry is not a project. It is an earnest attempt to sustain an existence at a proximity to the entire cosmos.

HUDA. Why did you choose *al-Ghazaliyya al-kubrā* (The Grand Ghazal) and *al-Shaẓāyā al-khamsumi'a* (The Five Hundred Fragments) for this volume?

SALIM. The excerpts I chose from *al-Ghazaliyya* are its backbone, the core of its structure. And those from *al-Shaẓāyā* are glimpses that I hoped would dazzle the English reader's imagination. I hope that one day, before I depart from this world, we'd translate an entire book-length poem like *al-Ālihah* (The Gods), for example. *Ajrafat al-mutajānis* (The Arrogance of Assonance) was translated into Swedish. In an elegant review of the translation, a Swedish poet advised his contemporaries to read and learn from it. Another book-length poem *Syria* was translated to Turkish. Who knows? Perhaps, you'll be the one to do this, Huda.

• ا اخترتُ فقراتٍ من العمود الفقري لـ " الغزلية الكبرى " الطويلة . لينها تُرجمت كاملة لا بأس . واخترتُ شذراتٍ من " الشظايا الخمسمائة " كومضٍ تعبّر خيال القارئ الانكليزي . ربما تُشّار ، يّلى الرحيل من الدنيا ، قصيدة كاملة كتابٍ ، مثل " آلهة " .

تُرجمت " عجرفة المتجانس " في كتابٍ بأكمله إلى السويدية . (نصحَ شاعرٌ سويديٌ أصحابه الشعراء ، في عرضه لكتابٍ الأنيق جداً ، أن " يتعلموا " منه) . قصيدة " سوريا " تُرجمت كاملة في كتابٍ بالتركية . من يدري . قد تفعلين ذلك يوماً ما ، اهدى .

سورية

'The excerpts I chose from al-Ghazaliyya ...'

108

HUDA. If *The Grand Ghazal* is a cathedral? What is its foundation and what are its extensions? What do you want to say about—or what do you want to do with—the ghazal as a genre in this work?

SALIM. *The Grand Ghazal* is simply the confessions of a lover, abundant and unbridled, creating an unprecedented ghazal that breaks free from borrowed conventions and exhausted language of the ghazal as we know it. It is a lover wandering in the cathedral of 'spiritual femininity', passionately seeking to capture the entirety of its design.

HUDA. And what about the feminine plural in *The Grand Ghazal* (for example, see p. 48, p. 72 in this volume). You know that it is a challenge in translation What do you mean by it? What effect do you seek from it?

SALIM. The feminine plural, what can I say? It is one of the Arabic language's conspiracies, dear Huda!

HUDA. Why did you choose to include excerpts from *Tandīd rūhānī* (A Spiritual Admonition)?

SALIM. I thought it held it place along with what we chose from the other works. I want these selections to all be short fragments or single lines.

HUDA. You said earlier that you prefer longer poems. With time, do you find yourself inclined towards shorter compositions?

SALIM. Not exactly. My forthcoming poetry collection *Maʿraka bi-tawqīt al-mā* (A Battle in Aquatime) is a book-length poem, but it is made of short, discrete parts. I like the precision and the complexity—the restrained complexity—of short compositions, even when they are parts of a longer work.

* * *

HUDA. Beirut gifted you many friendships. What remains of them today?

SALIM. I formed many strong friendships in Beirut, and all that my depths hold has come from there.

HUDA. Do you have friends you stay in touch with today?

SALIM. Besides my wife Cindy and my son Ran, I have very few friends. Only other exception is the Iraqi poet and novelist Walid Hermiz, who has diligently typed my work for the past eighteen years. We speak on the phone every two weeks. He lives in a city that's very far away. Surprisingly, have only met twice at the Gothenburg Book Fair—about twenty-three years ago, and then again twenty years ago.

Every year or so, I receive two guests—my Swedish translator, professor Jonathan Morén, and the founder and editor-in-chief of the well-regarded Swedish quarterly, *Karavan*, Birgitta Wallin. These are literally my only two guests.

HUDA. Where did you meet your wife?

SALIM. Cindy and I met in Cyprus. I had complimented her eyes and invited her to dinner, but she declined. I tried again a few months later, and this time she accepted. Here we are, thirty-five years later, still at that dinner and I'm still admiring her charming green eyes.

HUDA. What's the language you share with your son. Do you feel that like he knows you? Are you afraid of this distance between parents and children?

SALIM. We are a tribe of friends in this house. Ran has never called me 'Father', ever in his life. He just calls me by my name, bare on his tongue. I never asked him to or even hinted that he should abandon the word. But I'm happy. The word 'father' is an address of authority, patriarchy. And since his early adolescence, I have tried to be Ran's closest friend. There is utmost honesty between us. I listen to him, and he is discerning in his moral and social criticism. He has his own world, possessing abilities and tools I never had. He plays football, and is very good. He has a bunch of friends. I made him a wooden closet with my carpentry tools, to keep all his sports gear. He is a thirty-two now.

HUDA. Can you describe a day in your life, from morning to evening?

SALIM. I usually go to bed before midnight and wake up around seven in the morning. I take a shower before anything else, and then prepare breakfast for the three of us. Each of us prefers to eat something different for breakfast. At eight, I go out to shop in the city centre which is around twelve minutes away—I go shopping four days a week and stay home on the other days. When I return, I cook and catch up on the news and crimes of the world for about twenty minutes. Then I return to the book I'm reading, even if it's a book I'm reading for the third or fourth time. My reading options are dwindling.

At noon, I start writing, accompanied by a generous glass of whisky or a bottle of beer. Lunch is at one and usually accompanied by some music or silence. Cindy and Ran return late from work, so cook for them as well. Then I take a nap for around an hour and a half—a habit I've kept for many years, even during the Lebanese Civil War and against the sound of falling bombs.

After waking up, I exercise for an hour, then chat with Cindy or search for a new film or series to watch on TV. At four-thirty, I transcribe with a pen what I wrote with a pencil in the morning.

Dinner is at eight. It's the same every day—a piece of chicken without any accompaniments. I eat standing up and then wash the dishes. We have a dishwasher, but I've never used it. Instead, I've emptied it and is now a storage for beer.

Once I've washed all the dishes, not a spoon or fork left in the sink, I retire to my 'cave'. Each of us in the household has a separate evening routine, with our own TVs and nooks in the house.

It's 'boring' to those who fill their days with the noise obligations, social engagements and what not. But, for me, it is as full as can be. Every second of it is filled with lines that dance in my imagination like swarming fireflies. My day is a forest, and from a distance, only I can see that every tree in it is the dream of the tree next to it.

HUDA. When did your passion for cooking start? Tell me about your relationship with this type of composition?

SALIM. I began learning to cook in Cyprus. In Beirut, we lived in a building next to a restaurant owned by a friend, so I relied on them for food. However, when we moved to Cyprus, the capital of the island felt more like a village with only a few restaurants, and everything closed on the weekends. I started preparing simple meals and barbecued a lot. Even after we moved to Sweden, I continued to enjoy barbecuing. I still do it about once every week or two, and round the year. I have a shed in front of the house where I keep bags of coal and the barbecue tools. I also have a full carpentry set along with some paint buckets and brushes, so I can paint the house or work as a handyman carpenter if needed.

HUDA. Tell me more about your writing process? Do you have writing rituals?

SALIM. I don't have specific writing rituals or a structured writing routine. For me, a strong drink is enough to awaken the appetite for words, for devouring images and savouring meanings.

HUDA. In our correspondences, you handwrote all your responses. Is this how you always write, by hand? Why don't you consider other means of writing which might be more practical?

SALIM. I admit, Huda, that I regret my stubborn and deliberate resistance to writing on a machine. It would have saved me so much time and effort. However, there's no point in dwelling on regrets—it's too late now.

HUDA. How much time do you spend on revisions?

SALIM. I write with a pencil at noon, and I transcribe with a pen in the evening. Usually, what I write requires little editing.

HUDA. Does this differ between poetry and novels?

SALIM. To me, there is no difference between a poem and a novel except in length.

HUDA. Do your publishers intervene in the text? Do you consider their suggestions if they offer any?

SALIM. No publisher has ever intervened in my text, since the very first book. No one has offered suggestions. Even the book covers, I design them all myself.

HUDA. Do you consult with anyone on your drafts and take their opinions into account?

SALIM. My loneliness is my only counsellor. I consult it and follow its advice.

HUDA. Is there a text that you still dream of writing?

SALIM. I don't have a specific text in mind that I dream of. I write first, and then I dream. I dream of my characters as they venture beyond my novel, pursuing their dreams in their own worlds. As for poetry . . . to write poetry is to swim in the explosion of the universe.

HUDA. Is there something you are still waiting for?

SALIM. What is life but waiting, and we are its creatures—the ones who wait and the ones who are awaited

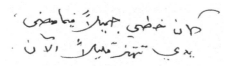

'My handwriting used to be beautiful.
Nowadays, my hand shakes a little.'

Translator's Acknowledgements

Special thanks to Cindy Inglessis for her patience, warmth, and help in facilitating our communication, and to antón shammás for reading an early draft of this translation and offering invaluable feedback.